Joash's Influences
Lessons About Following Friends

Thomas Murosky, Ph.D.
Kings of All Creation Series Vol 3

© 2022 by Thomas Murosky, Ph.D.

Published by Our Walk in Christ Publishing
State College, PA
www.owicpub.com

All rights reserved. No part of this publication may be reproduced, distributed, or transmitted in any form or by any means, including photocopying, recording, or other electronic or mechanical methods, without the prior written permission of the publisher, except in the case of brief quotations embodied in critical reviews and certain other noncommercial uses permitted by copyright law.

Joash's Influences: Lessons About Following Friends

First Printing 2022
ISBN: 978-1-7348398-8-3 (sc)
ISBN: 978-1-7348398-9-0 (e)

Scripture quotations taken from the New American Standard Bible® (NASB95), Copyright © 1960, 1962, 1963, 1968, 1971, 1972, 1973, 1975, 1977, 1995 by The Lockman Foundation. Used by permission. www.lockman.org

The Internet addresses in this book are accurate at the time of publication. They are provided as a resource, but due to the nature of the Internet, those addresses may change.

Commitment to Open Source: Our Walk in Christ Publishing uses FOSS software where available. This book was produced with LibreOffice, GNU Image Manipulator Program, Sigil, and the following open fonts: Charis SIL, PlainBlack, and DejaVu Sans. Chapter dividers obtained from https://openclipart.org. Audiobook edition produced with Audacity and Kid3.

LCCN: 2022950813

Dedication

This book is dedicated to the many students I mentored over the years in hopes they will see the truth in the pages of Scripture and see that true salvation comes from following God, not people.

Acknowledgments

I wish to acknowledge my followers and readers in my online communities for the encouragement to continue writing and teaching across the spectrum of the Christian faith. Thanks for watching and reading. Please stay in touch!

I also wish to acknowledge my financial backers who have provided support allowing me to spend more time researching, learning, and writing on Christian topics. Without your support, I could not release these books.

Thanks to Tyler for the thoughts and beta read, and to Kate for doing the final round of editing.

Finally, thanks to you, my readers, who make putting my thoughts on paper, digital ink, and audio tracks worth the while! I pray that my experiences while growing in my faith will help you grow as you walk in Christ.

Table of Contents

Table of Contents 6
Introduction 7
Learning Objectives 13
Joash: A Kingdom in Conflict 21
Shifting Influences 31
The Importance of Influences 39
Our Ultimate Choice 51
Real Salvation 67
Create Your Personal Plan 81
The Gospel 93
Bibliography 95
Scripture Index 96

Introduction

High school was a rough time. Like many of you out there, my relationship with my parents waned while hormones were infecting my mind with all sorts of things that I loved... and hated... and hated to love. This conflict in all of us seeks our counsel, and often we find that counsel in the all the wrong places.

In my case, I had two specific influences in my early years of high school that sought to push me in two different directions. One of these influences found their enjoyment in all the titillating carnal pleasures that the Devil offers. He was into drugs of all kinds, even boasting to have tried every single drug, because, "without trying them, you have no right to say why you shouldn't do them." He was into homosexuality before it was in vogue, and his whole life centered on a perpetual party. If he had his way, I would be his disciple in sin. I would have experimented with strange sex, and burned out my mind on godless pharmaceuticals.

My other influence had also lived on the wild side of life. In contrast, such life experiences matured him beyond his years. While he was a decade younger than the older man, his advice was more sage than the fool who sought to experiment with all forms of sin.

During those turbulent times, I thought it would be cool to pick up smoking. I asked an older friend to buy me a pack of smokes, so I, too, could slip them into my amazing leather jacket that set me apart from the rest of the school. Of course, all the kids in our cool clique wore the leather jacket, grew our hair long, and usually wore shirts that frightened the good people of the world. Even my mom insisted that I not wear the T-shirt of the demon ripping the skeleton apart for her upcoming wedding, so I went with the skull T-shirt instead. All the friends in our group duplicated this model to differ from everyone else in school, but we kept each other in line with our code of awesome.

At the end of the school week, my best friend, who had moved to another district, came over as usual. I lit up, and he made fun of me for my stupid new habit of smoking. His peer pressure convinced me that my new habit was horrible, so I tossed the rest of the smokes into my brother's room and never puffed a cigarette again. This little parable shows us everything we need to know about influences.

Influences can be positive or negative. They can lead us into the best decisions we could ever make, or they can direct us down the worst paths our hearts and minds could lead us. We are rarely islands unto ourselves, and we often take our cues from others. For kids who grow up with exemplary parents and homes, their folks usually direct them in the right ways *(Proverbs 22:6)*, but for those out there like myself, our peer group became our cruel teacher.

In this short book, we will look at the personal influences in our life and what they mean for our walk with God. We will examine what true salvation means. Further, we will ask if we really are saved, or if we look like saved believers because of our circle of friends. After all, the adage is true: Going into church doesn't mean you are saved any more than going into a garage means you are a car.

Herein, we will learn the lessons of true salvation from Joash, an Old Testament king. We will see how he gave every appearance of salvation as long as his mentor, the high priest Jehoida, lived. But we will also see his truly spectacular fall as he shifted his attention to his friends and adopted their foolish counsel.

We will ask what is true salvation? Did we really get saved at five years old during the Vacation Bible School altar call after being told by the nice lady dressed in a clown suit that we have to choose between heaven or hell? Maybe we were saved after the thirty-seventh time of walking forward or raising our hands to accept Jesus at the end of the church service. Humbly still, possibly we are deceiving ourselves into thinking our salvation is real when in reality we are truly lost. After all, Jesus said that many are deceived in the terrifying discourse on the Sermon on the Mount:

> *Not everyone who says to Me, 'Lord, Lord,' will enter the kingdom of heaven, but he who does the will of My Father who is in heaven will enter. Many will say to Me on that day, 'Lord, Lord, did we not prophesy in Your name, and in Your name cast out demons, and in*

Your name perform many miracles?' And then I will declare to them, 'I never knew you; depart from Me, you who practice lawlessness (Matthew 7:21-23).'

So what does it mean to be saved? And how can we know we are saved? King Joash gave every sign of salvation, but when the end of his life came, it would appear that he never really knew God. How can we avoid his trap and know for certain that we are truly following God? I will answer these questions in this book.

1
Learning Objectives

Our character can be determined by the company we keep. Our friendships, our counsel give us the direction for our lives, and we will see from the life of Joash (some translations use Johoash in some references to this king) that during one phase of his life, God blessed him and called him a righteous king. During another phase, God called him wicked and judged him. The difference was a shift in Joash's circle of influence. This should be enough for us to pause and reflect on our own influences. But we will see in this chapter that there is more to salvation than the company we keep.

Why Are Influences So Important?

None of us is an island unto ourselves. As a human race, God created us to desire companionship and fellowship. We create tribes based on what is common to us. Consider the miraculous event when God came down and confused the language of the Babylonians.

> Come, let Us go down and there confuse their language, so that they will not understand one another's speech." So the Lord scattered them abroad from there over the face of the whole earth; and they stopped building the city. Therefore its name was called Babel, because there the Lord confused the language of the whole earth; and from there the Lord scattered them abroad over the face of the whole earth (Genesis 11:7-9).

The people split into different groups from which the various races that we know today had evolved. The groups assembled into what united them: a common tongue.

United around speech, each member of society created a system by which to hold all others accountable. People then adopted their own mindsets, tendencies, and even the traits we call "stereotypes" today. Consider the stereotype that arose out of the

Learning Objectives

island of Crete. There is a word in our dictionary, cretin (someone of coarse character), which is derived from some attitudes that the people of that island held. Paul referenced the stereotype of the people of Crete as a reason to exhort the people more harshly:

> *One of themselves, a prophet of their own, said, "Cretans are always liars, evil beasts, lazy gluttons." This testimony is true. For this reason reprove them severely so that they may be sound in the faith, not paying attention to Jewish myths and commandments of men who turn away from the truth (Titus 1:12-14).*

The group holds its members together and the person, generally speaking, becomes identified by the circles they move around in.

We see Jehoiada had influenced Joash, who was like a parent figure to the new king. The power dynamic here plays itself out by causing "better" behavior in the child, but the genuine test is how does he behave when no one is looking? Here, when his "daddy" turned his head, Joash ran with a rough crowd of his peers. When the time came for Joash to rule the kingdom on his own, he turned to the wrong counsel and made decisions that caused God to judge him. Here, the power dynamics of friends often cause us to move to the extremes of destructive behavior that we would not typically do if left to ourselves.

When we have positive influences in our lives, we tend to move toward positive morality, but when our circle of friends is into many sins found in the fruit of the flesh *(Galatians 5:19-21)*, it is not a surprise that sin becomes easier. Thus, examining our influences is a primary learning objective in this chapter.

Finding The Right Influences

Our next aim will be to spend some time learning how to evaluate our influences and seek out the people who can help us the most.

Growing up, many of us may have had friends of whom our parents disapproved. While we may have fought against such censorship of our friends, our parents had our best interests in mind. They knew that if we started surrounding ourselves with hoodlums as friends that we would likely become a troublemaker. This early training helped us shape the way we look at friendships, but it is a lesson that some of us may have forgotten. Here we will talk about what types of people we should surround ourselves with, who we minister to, and who we let minister to us.

Ultimately, we all choose our friends and the people who influence us in life. It is best if we honestly examine the fruit of their life and determine if this is a person we would like to emulate.

We will look at tips for finding friends, how to identify who is best to spend time with, and how to break off friendships with people who we may need to let go of. Our lesson here is not to excise all the non-believers in our life, but how to be sober-minded in approaching friendships.

The Desire To Know God

We will see from Joash that the most important lesson is not the people who influence us in life, but how close we are to God. Ultimately, as we will see, God did not judge Joash for picking bad friends. He judged the king for his own failure to follow God with all his heart, mind, soul, and strength.

The question remains, and we shall examine it more later, what is our draw to God or the world?

Joash's Influences

Picture, if you will, a balance. On each bucket is a cup. If we spend most of our time with God, and we find that the Bible and the impressions he makes in our heart guide us, the scale tips toward God, and we generally become more like Him. But if we spend much more time with friends, their cup fills more and the scale bends in that way, causing us to follow in their ways. If your friends are also listening to God, you will always be drawn closer to Him. But if they are people of the world, they can lead you astray. Again, we will consider these principles more closely later.

The final and most important question we will examine in this book will be whether you are doing Christian things because of your circle of friends, or if you are doing them because of your personal relationship with God. This makes all the difference in your eternal destination, as we have seen in the introduction that many people think they are going to heaven when, in fact, Jesus says that He never knew them *(Matthew 7:21-23)*.

We will ask questions to get us thinking about whether we are truly saved or if we attend Christian functions because of our family or the expectations imposed on us by the world. Start thinking about that question now.

Chapter Summary

Our learning objectives for this book will be **to ask who is influencing us. Is that influence meaningful for our eternity?** While the influences in our lives are important, they are not as important as the final question we will ask: **Are we really following God with all our heart, mind, soul, and strength**, or are we just putting on a show of the habit, expectation, or self-deception. These are the significant questions we will ask in this book.

2
Joash: A Kingdom in Conflict

"Yet even now," declares the Lord,
"Return to Me with all your heart,
And with fasting, weeping and mourning;
And rend your heart and not your garments."
Now return to the Lord your God,
For He is gracious and compassionate,
Slow to anger, abounding in lovingkindness
And relenting of evil.
Who knows whether He will not turn and relent
And leave a blessing behind Him,
Even a grain offering and a drink offering
For the Lord your God?
(Joel 2:12-14)

Joash didn't become king in usual succession. It was typical for the son to start a co-regency with his father, and when the father passed, the reign would seamlessly transition to the new king. But Joash came to power differently. He was the true king, the seed of David, and rightful heir to the throne. The rest of his family line, however, had been extinguished.

While Joash was part of the royal line, he was also part of Ahab's line. Ahab, in fact, is his great-grandfather. You may remember Ahab as the most wicked king in Israel's history up unto his time, only being surpassed in debauchery by Manasseh a few generations later. He was the evil king who let his wife, Jezebel, destroy all the prophets in the land while allowing Baal and Asherah to be worshiped freely *(1 Kings 16:31-33, 1 Kings 18:3)*.

Ahab's evil kingdom included enough drama to be featured on the latest shock talk show, complete with betrayals, murders, usurping, and more. It was a period in Israel's history where worship of the true God had been lost and even criminalized. Meanwhile, the family lines between the northern and southern kingdoms became intertwined and the plan to eliminate David's root almost became reality. But Joash was saved from

Joash: A Kingdom in Conflict

death by a priest who knew of the one true God and an aunt who had compassion for a newly born baby.

Generations In Conflict

The conflict surrounding Joash's kingdom starts with his great-grandfather, Ahab. This king and his wicked wife, Jezebel, led the northern kingdom into Baal worship. It was not merely adding Baal to the regime of worship, but persecuting the true worshipers. The wicked palace authorities put to death the true worshipers so much so that Elijah even believed he was the last prophet left *(1 Kings 19:10)*.

Ahab was credited as one of the worse kings in the northern kingdom, but even he repented in his lifetime. He died in battle *(2 Kings 22:34)* and his son, Ahaziah, became king *(1 Kings 22:40)*. He was as evil as his father, and only survived two years before dying childless, so his brother, Jehoram (sometimes translated as Joram) became king *(2 Kings 1:17)*.

While this drama was unfolding in the northern kingdom, Jehoshaphat ruled in the southern kingdom. While he was a righteous king, following the commands of God, he made alliances with Ahab's family, which became an influence leading Judah into sin *(1 Kings 29:44, 2 Kings 22:29)*. It was possibly this alliance that caused Judah to fall into the false worship which would eventually lead them into exile *(Ezekiel 23:11)*.

While Jehoshaphat followed God, his son, Jehoram (a different Jehoram than Ahab's son) was not as righteous. The family alliances that his father forged led him to marry Athialiah, the wicked daughter of Ahab and Jezebel. She led Judah into sin *(2 Kings 8:18)*. Their son, Ahaziah, named for his uncle, also followed the ways of Baal *(2 Kings 8:25-27)*.

God didn't sit idly by while idolatry took over the nation. Back in the era of Ahab and Jezebel, when Baal worship reached its peak, God had told Elijah the prophet parts of his plan to destroy Baal worship in the land:

> *The Lord said to him, "Go, return on your way to the wilderness of Damascus, and when you have arrived, you shall anoint Hazael king over Aram; and Jehu the son of Nimshi you shall anoint king over Israel; and Elisha the son of Shaphat of Abel-*

meholah you shall anoint as prophet in your place. It shall come about, the one who escapes from the sword of Hazael, Jehu shall put to death, and the one who escapes from the sword of Jehu, Elisha shall put to death. Yet I will leave 7,000 in Israel, all the knees that have not bowed to Baal and every mouth that has not kissed him (1 Kings 19:15-18)."

The plan included a continuation of his ministry through Elisha, and using the king of Syria (Aram) to weaken the two kingdoms. Once the wicked Israelites suffered a few defeats, Jehu would be anointed king of Israel in a coup to kill Ahab's line *(2 Kings 9:6-10)*.

The Root Of Jessie

This brings us to Joash, the son of Ahaziah, the son of Jehoram *(2 Kings 11:2)*. Athialiah was his grandmother. When Jehu overtook Jehoram, the king of Israel, and Ahaziah, the king of Judah, Athialiah usurped the throne of Judah and started executing the royal family, which mostly comprised her own grandchildren *(2 Kings 11:1)*. Her daughter, Jehosheba, hid her nephew, Joash, in the temple so that the wicked queen couldn't destroy him. Joash was the last surviving member of King David's family line, and the single remaining true heir to the throne of both the kingdom, but also of the line of the coming Messiah.

Joash was entrusted to the priest Jehoiada. He remained hidden in the temple for seven years, but on reaching the age of seven, he was anointed and proclaimed as king over Judah *(2 Kings 11:4-12)*.

Athialiah heard the commotion and went into the temple to see the king she had failed to destroy standing there. She attempted to call her last followers, but the loyal subjects executed her instead *(2 Kings 11:13-16)*. From that day, they extinguished Baal worship in Israel.

Prophets In Joash's Time

God spoke to the Israelites in several ways throughout the generations. In the earliest of times, he spoke to Abraham, Joseph, and Moses. Of course, Moses was the only person God ever talked to "face to face" *(Deuteronomy 34:10)*. After Moses and Joshua died, the people did what they thought was right *(Judges 21:25)*. Judges who passed on knowledge of God ruled them, and of course, the priests had that

Joash: A Kingdom in Conflict

role, though some strayed from the truth. In the time of Samuel, the last judge, the people asked for a king *(1 Samuel 8:1-9)*. They were given a king to rule over them and from that period, the king and priests spoke for God. Of course there were some prophets in the land in those days, but we have little record of them. One such prophet was Nathan, whom confronted David *(2 Samuel 12:1-15)*. Gad also talked to David *(1 Samuel 22:5)*, Ahijah prophesied in the time of Solomon *(1 Kings 11:29)*. Most of these prophets seemed to have minor roles in the kingdom.

But in the days of Ahab, they put the prophets to death by Jezebel's command, and Elijah rose as a powerful voice for God. He marks the first in the line of prophets, which changed their role in giving basic guidance to the king to speaking about God's judgment that was coming to the land for their disobedience.

The next three prophets in the land, after Elijah all prophesied during the days of Joash. The first was Elisha, the successor to Elijah. This powerful prophet raised people from the dead, confronted entire kingdoms and oversaw the fulfillment of Elijah's commission to put to death Ahab's line and abolish Baal worship from the land.

Obadiah also prophesied, but mostly to Edom, about their destruction for their battles with Israel. This little book gives us some clarity to how God will curse those who curse Israel *(Genesis 12:3)*.

Joel prophesied to the southern kingdom with a message focusing on the judgment of God for their sins. The Israelites are experiencing judgment in the form of a locust swarm consuming their crops. That is just what Moses warned: *You shall bring out much seed to the field but you will gather in little, for the locust will consume it (Deuteronomy 28:38).* Joel brings them back to the promises of God that if they turn to Him, he will bless them, but if they turn away, He will curse them. This all happens at a time when the people have turned from God to worship Baal instead.

Chapter Summary

Joash inherited a kingdom in shambles from the sin and deceit in the kingdom. The sin that started in his great-grandfather's time threatened to wipe out the entire nation. He alone was saved as the last descendant of David, and his kingdom was established under God. But we will see soon how he didn't trust in God as much as the people who influenced his life.

3
Shifting Influences

But I will remove the northern army far from you,
And I will drive it into a parched and desolate land,
And its vanguard into the eastern sea,
And its rear guard into the western sea.
And its stench will arise and its foul smell will come up,
For it has done great things.
(Joel 2:20)

Joash began his kingship at seven years old. Like all kids, he followed the ways of his de facto parents. Here, his real mother and father were dead, but Jehoiada the priest was his acting authority. We read in *2 Kings 12:2* that *Jehoash (Joash) did right in the sight of the Lord all his days in which Jehoiada the priest instructed him.* Sadly, though, he didn't really seek to follow god, especially since the unlawful places to worship remained in his days *(2 Kings 12:3)*.

Life Under Jehoiada

Jehoiada was a priest after God's heart. He knew the law and did his best to make sure the people followed God in the days of his life. Jehoida first tasked Joash in making sure the people followed the ways of God:

> *Then Jehoiada made a covenant between himself and all the people and the king, that they would be the Lord's people (2 Chronicles 23:16).*

On the day that Joash took over the kingdom and his guard slayed Athaliah, the faithful subjects killed the Baal worshipers and destroyed the house of Baal *(2 Chronicles 23:17)*.

But this idolatrous house wasn't the only concern. The temple had been polluted by the evil kings preceding Joash, and Athaliah's priests used the sacred items in the temple for Baal worship *(2 Chronicles 24:7)*. Joash asked the priests to clean it up and repair the temple, but their corruption kept them from the task *(2 Chronicles 14:4-7)*. Joash built a chest for the worshipers to donate to the repair fund and only allowed the workers to take money from it as needed for the work. This plan allowed the workers to repair, and the people returned to worshiping the Lord.

The Foolish Counsel

Joash didn't fully follow God. In fact, evidence suggests he didn't follow God at all, but simply followed Jehoiada. Once the old priest died, Joash's friends came around and gave him counsel which differed from the priest. *2 Chronicles 24:17-18* gives us the stunning reversal:

> *But after the death of Jehoiada the officials of Judah came and bowed down to the king, and the king listened to them. They abandoned the house of the Lord, the God of their fathers, and served the Asherim and the idols; so wrath came upon Judah and Jerusalem for this their guilt.*

All the positive that Joash had done in the land under Jehoiada didn't last. Joash didn't follow God for himself. He did it because he felt a loyalty to Jehoiada. Once his mentor and long-time friend left the kingdom,

Joash's Influences

Joash turned away from God and toward the idols of his father's sin.

Joash's past blessings departed him as he turned to Baal worship. God had tried to turn him back by sending prophets, including Zechariah, the son of Jehoiada to Priest. God reminded Joash of His laws, but the king didn't care. Instead, he sent his men to execute Zechariah. They spilled his blood in the sanctuary's courtyard *(2 Chronicles 24:20-22)*. Zechariah called out judgment on him in his dying breath:

> *May the Lord see and avenge!*
> *(2 Chronicles 24:22)*

God heard the words of the fallen prophet. His proclamation of curses recorded in *Deuteronomy 28:25* came true. A small army of Arameans defeated Joash in battle *(2 Chronicles 24:23-24)*. God destroyed the wicked advisors, and Joash died at the hands of his own servants, a punishment he earned for himself by executing Zechariah *(2 Chronicles 24:25)*.

When Joash died, his subjects didn't even honor him enough to bury him in the tombs of the kings. In the final years of his life, God removed His blessings from the king and the land, causing them to be defeated by their enemies. Finally, Joash became despicable to his people. This comes to people who reject God.

Taking Stock Of Our Influences

Joash's fall happened when he rejected God and the instruction of his mentor to listen to his advisors instead. This isn't the first time we see advisors lead a king down the wrong path. Rehoboam came to power after Solomon and his answer to the people split the kingdom. The people came to him after the death of his father, Solomon, and asked for their workload to be reduced. The elders gave this answer:

> Then they spoke to him, saying, "If you will be a servant to this people today, and will serve them and grant them their petition, and speak good words to them, then they will be your servants forever (1 Kings 12:7)."

Rehoboam chose not to listen to the elder advisors and listened to the young men who grew up with him. This is what the king said to the people:

Joash's Influences

> *My father made your yoke heavy, but I will add to your yoke; my father disciplined you with whips, but I will discipline you with scorpions (1 Kings 12:14).*

When the people didn't have their way, and considering the harsh way that Rehoboam spoke to them, the northern territories left behind David's kingdom and returned to following Saul's family line. The kingdoms split on that day and they remained divided until the intertestimental period.

Let this be a lesson to you about whom you allow to influence you in your life. Consider first the lessons you may have learned from your children. If they ever found a friend whom was a little rough around the edges, you may have noticed your child also becoming a little rowdy. The old saying is true: show me your friends, and I'll show you the type of person you will soon become.

Sometimes we find friends that are truly positive. They may guide us back on track with God. If you found friends that encourage you to read your Bible, work in some form of mission field, or return to church, you have found a good friend that will guide you in the right directions.

Your friends, however, can neither save you nor condemn you. We all stand before God on our own. He is our master and judge *(Romans 14:4)*. Whether we stand or fall depends solely on whether we truly trust Jesus with our salvation. A positive influence can bring us to the cross of Christ, but we must follow Him for ourselves. Likewise, a negative influence can cause us to displease our God, but no one is able to rip us loose from the hands of our savior *(John 10:27-29)*.

The Best True Influence

The best influence is a person who points us to God. The Scriptures lay out many directives for us to influence one another. First, a positive influence encourages us into love and good deeds *(Hebrews 10:23-24)*. They pray for us regarding our sins and well-being *(James 5:16)*. A beneficial influence lives out their life as a Christian and is not merely a person who goes to church because they are supposed to. Being called to Christ is a lifestyle, and not an obligation.

Joash's Influences

Joash viewed following God as an obligation that he had to perform as long as Jehoiada lived, but once the old priest died, his true colors and devotion revealed themselves.

Chapter Summary

Joash did all that Jehoida commanded until his death, so he was said to **follow God all the days of Jehoiada**. But once the priest died, Joash listened to his friends instead, and that meant a return to worshiping idols. **While his influences cannot save him or condemn him**, they pointed him to God on the one hand, and Satan on the other. We can say the same for our influences, and that means **it is important to consider who we allow to speak into our life**.

4
The Importance of Influences

*Then you will know that I am the Lord your God,
Dwelling in Zion, My holy mountain.
So Jerusalem will be holy,
And strangers will pass through it no more.
(Joel 3:17)*

No man is an island unto himself. Well, at least not people who dwell among and interact with society. Whether it is the music we hear or the movies we see, we're never without influence. But the most important factor in our influences are the people in our lives.

Growing up, we may have had a friend whom our parents didn't like. "He is a bad influence on you," my mom told me of my best friend from the 8th grade. Looking back, she was right in that he wasn't the best influence I could have, but at least he wasn't the one who "influenced" my teenage hoodlum arrest! But in all seriousness, we needn't blame our parents or friends when they decry our relationship choices because God said it first:

> *Do not be deceived:*
> *"Bad company corrupts good morals."*
> *(1 Corinthians 15:33)*

Good And Bad

I'm reminded here of two episodes from Adventures in Odyssey that dealt with the subject of friends and influences. In *The Good, The Bad, & Butch*[1], two old friends reunite, but one of them has joined the mischievous gang around town. As the two remember their old innocent childhood friendship, they clash over the fact that Butch wants to bring Sam into the gang and include him in their mischievous pranks. Likewise, Sam tries to bring Butch back to church. In the end, the kids part ways. Butch goes back to his mischief, and Sam goes back to his youth group.

Rarely, however, is that how friendships play out in real life.

Of course, the Adventures in Odyssey series is a long-running story and in a future mini-series, Butch helps the good guys when the gang around town is taking part in a vandalism scheme. This shows us that when we stand our ground on morality, sometimes people come around. It didn't happen quickly, but it happened after a period of Sam returning to his positive influences and Butch realizing his gang friends were not leading him down the right path.

The character of Butch here is a magnificent case study in the human nature. By default, we are all sinners. We like the sin and the evil. We may not like the long-term consequences, but at the moment, no one can say that some sins do not seem 'fun'. But in this case, Sam shines a light on his friend and Butch sees how wicked he is. He runs from the light to consider it privately for a while. This is just as Jesus said in *John 3:19*:

> *This is the judgment, that the Light has come into the world, and men loved the darkness rather than the Light, for their deeds were evil.*

The second episode, *Under the Influence*[2], represents a better illustration that people usually find themselves in. Aubrey is floundering in life, asking questions about the meaning of it all. When her old friend, Erica, moves to town. The two reunite, but Erica subtly pushes Aubrey into rebellious ways. By the end of the first part in the two-part episode, Aubrey is talking, acting, and deceiving, like Erica. The discipleship was complete until Erica went too far, jarring Aubrey out of the influence.

In real life, we rarely get out of the influence so quickly, nor is it often easy to just change course. Rather, we assimilate the new behaviors into our own life slowly. For this reason, we need to be very cautious about whom we let influence us. After all, we are naturally social creatures who want to belong to a group, and we will do things to belong that we may not do if left to ourselves.

The Importance of Influences

We need to seek people who can help and mentor us. The best approach is to think about the life we would like to live and find people who are already living it. Sometimes you can get real time with people (this is more preferred), but you can also pick up a lot of tips from reading, listening, and watching what they do from books, videos, and articles.

How Our Influences Affect Us

Gardeners know plants are ripening or decaying. Our lives are much the same way. As we grow in faith and maturity, we are always moving toward ripening, or growing in our Godly character *(2 Peter 1:5-8)*. Otherwise, we decay into the sins of the flesh *(Galatians 5:19-21)*. Our personal relationships are the fertilizer for our growth or decay that manifests as the behavior we exhibit in life.

Our examples from Adventures in Odyssey illustrate for us a few ways where relationships either help or hinder us. On the one hand, a positive influence can enter our life and move us toward Godliness. The author of Hebrews commands us to seek such relationships to encourage one another into the deeds of righteousness:

> *Let us consider how to stimulate one another to love and good deeds (Hebrews 10:24).*

Being humans and sinners by nature, however, when confronted with bad influences in our life, we generally adopt the ways of the flesh more than we internalize the fruit of the spirit. We are truly open books on how influence impacts us. After a long day of work, we can drift toward the influences of sin in a wicked television program or website. But if we catch ourselves, we can turn instead to entertainment or endeavors that will draw us closer to God instead. Therefore, Scripture warns us to be careful about where we place our attention:

> *Sow with a view to righteousness, reap in accordance with kindness; break up your fallow ground, for it is time to seek the Lord until He comes to rain righteousness on you. You have plowed wickedness, you have reaped injustice, you have eaten the fruit of lies. Because you have trusted in your way, in your numerous warriors, therefore a tumult will arise among your people, and all your fortresses will be destroyed, as Shalman destroyed Beth-arbel on the day of battle,*

when mothers were dashed in pieces with their children (Hosea 10:12-14).

If we spend our time sowing into our flesh and the worldly desires that come with it, we find ourselves being corrupted to the core. But the time we spend seeking God, we are growing closer to him.

With the warnings about why we need to be careful about sowing to the flesh instead of the spirit, Paul instructs us again to live righteously in the present age *(Titus 2:12)*. This is very important because our life is the strongest of ministries we can have, but our failures can cause people to despise God more than anything else.

Our Need For Christian Fellowship

We need Christian fellowship. Without believers around us, we wither and die under the influence of the world. We mentioned in the prior section the Bible instructs us to encourage one another into good deeds. The very next verse reminds us:

Not forsaking our own assembling together, as is the habit of some, but encouraging one another;

and all the more as you see the day drawing near (Hebrews 10:25).

Most people use this verse as the ultimate justification to skip fishing on Sunday morning to attend the worship service instead. It is important to attend church, but the verse is far more important than an admonition to use Sunday mornings for worship. It is a verse about the lifestyle of the Christian, always encouraging one another into good deeds and always seeking fellowship.

Having brought up the word "fellowship" I think it merits a discussion here. This is a commonly Christianized word often co-opted to mean a group of people from the church meeting up. Usually, however, such groups talk about everything except God. Real fellowship is an extraction of this section of Hebrews: Get together regularly, pray for one another, encourage one another into good deeds. Fellowship is explicitly a gathering to encourage one another in the faith, not a time to talk about football statistics and social acumen.

Consider what happened in the early foundations of the church. In *Acts 2:42*, all the people were joining in with the believers continually. They had fellowship over the words and teachings of the apostles. They ate meals together, and they prayed continually. And this was the practice every day, not only on Sunday mornings. It was a continual process as they lived their lives.

The relationships they forged as they learned what it meant to follow God helped them during the times of persecution. We see the people didn't reject God; they scattered abroad. When they did, fellowship gave them the knowledge to preach the word as they went *(Acts 8:4)*.

When they reached new towns and preached the Gospel of Christ, they formed additional groups of believers in every city and they carried on the traditions they learned in Jerusalem. Christians met together in houses, tombs, fields, and other places they could just to spend time with one another growing in Christ, praying, eating together, and living life always, not just on Sunday morning. In short, they guarded their influences.

Influences And Godly Decisions

Our discussion of influences in this chapter raises the famous "chicken and egg" question. Are we Godly because we made righteous decisions about our friends and associations or do we associate with people who are Godly themselves because of our position with God? This question is at the heart of our influences, and the answer is that we choose our friends based on the overflow of our hearts. That means when we hang out with someone new, our spirits will either connect or we go away thinking that we want those hours back for ourselves. This illustrates our selection of friends based on the convictions in our hearts.

This means that we connect with people that are most similar to us. The expression, "show me your friends, and I'll show you your character," is true in the sense that we do not *become* our friends... we adopt the friends we have based on our heart. So when you look up and see vile people in your circle of influence, it merits asking yourself if these are the people you connect with because they are the people you are. This is why I adopted the dress patterns of my friends in

The Importance of Influences

high school, and why we begin resembling our cliques more and more. Think about the people who best honor God. If we assimilate with those people, we will adopt the characteristics of a person who honors God.

In this sense, we see Joash followed God for the days that Jehoiada was alive because he followed his mentor and father figure. He did things like repair the temple (*2 Kings 12:4-8*) because he knew it would please Jehoiada.

We see, however, that after Jehoiada died, Joash had the opportunity to continue a relationship with his son, Zechariah. This man was godly and also the high priest under his reign. Joash followed his friends, who were godless *(2 Chronicles 24:17-18)* and murdered Zechariah *(2 Chronicles 24:22)*. This ultimate betrayal of his lifelong friend ultimately illustrated that Joash wasn't a godly man at all.

Obviously, we all know people who are not walking with God, and that is OK. But when we consider the core group of people allowed to speak into our lives, those should also be following Jesus the best they can. The rest of the world is indeed our mission field, but we should not let them guide our thoughts and decisions on a day-to-day basis.

Take care to learn a lesson from Joash: if you find yourself surrounded by godless people, ask yourself if you really know God. Seek Him with all your heart and find out if your inner circle knows Him in the same way you do.

Chapter Summary

The people we choose to spend time with **ultimately bring us closer to God or draw us away**. It is important to always be thinking about our friendships and inner circle of friends. **Those people should be our fellowship partners**. If we find people who are not walking with God, pause and **ask if we surround ourselves with such people because we are struggling with God ourselves**.

5
Our Ultimate Choice

Multitudes, multitudes in the valley of decision!
For the day of the Lord is near in the valley of decision.
(Joel 3:14)

Joash had the option to follow God through Jehoiada's son, but he opted instead to follow worthless men. While we may not rule a kingdom or have command over an entire country, we make life choices about whom to follow, and that will affect the course of our lives. Joshua set the decision about whom to follow before the people:

> *Now, therefore, fear the Lord and serve Him in sincerity and truth; and put away the gods which your fathers served beyond the River and in Egypt, and serve the Lord. If it is disagreeable in your sight to serve the Lord, choose for yourselves today whom you will serve: whether the gods which your fathers served which were beyond the River, or the gods of the Amorites in whose land you are living; but as for me and my house, we will serve the Lord (Joshua 24:14-15).*

We likewise need to make that choice in our lives. Are we going to serve God and allow His people to speak into our lives? Or are we going to follow our wicked and fleshy heart?

Old And New Testament Consequences

An age-old theological debate centers about the context and ability for man to have free will. Some argue there is no free will at all. I would reject this premise as not being biblical. If we have no free will at all, God directs all decisions and becomes the author of sin in the lives of men. This is the theological error called **fatalism**. The Bible gives us a few clues about the interplay between men's plans and God's direction.

> *The mind of man plans his way,*
> *But the Lord directs his steps.*
> *(Proverbs 16:9)*

We see from this proverb that we have plans and directions, but God's sovereignty always moves us in the way that matches His plan. When we do not focus on God's ways, the plan we devise for our lives and the plan God devises deviates, and He sets the universe in motion to bring us in alignment with His plans.

Our Ultimate Choice

The teaching from a Calvinist like myself will suggest that man has free will, but his will cannot choose to follow God without Him first working in our heart *(John 6:44)*. Ultimately, this usually means that man selects the nature and severity of his sin. To illustrate, every night we come home tired and face a choice. We can study our Bible or watch the news, for example. When selecting a movie, we can watch a film that glorifies God or one that does not. Ultimately, however, what we watch or read does not send us to heaven or hell. But the patterns in our lives are the manifestation of the possible destiny of our soul, but the finished work of Christ caused salvation on the cross.

The natural man tends to make decisions moving him toward the flesh, and when that happens, he reaps the fruit of the flesh. Paul warns in *Galatians 6:7-8*:

> *Do not be deceived, God is not mocked; for whatever a man sows, this he will also reap. For the one who sows to his own flesh will from the flesh reap corruption, but the one who sows to the Spirit will from the Spirit reap eternal life.*

He illustrated earlier in the letter what corruption of the flesh looks like:

> Now the deeds of the flesh are evident, which are: immorality, impurity, sensuality, idolatry, sorcery, enmities, strife, jealousy, outbursts of anger, disputes, dissensions, factions, envying, drunkenness, carousing, and things like these, of which I forewarn you, just as I have forewarned you, that those who practice such things will not inherit the kingdom of God (Galatians 5:19-21).

When confronted with decisions in life, we need to set aside the debate about whether God is a fatalist or if we are actually the ones making decisions about our lives. **We need to recognize that when we fight against the spirit, we are already corrupted in the flesh.**

These are not just New Testament principles. Joash had a copy of the law *(2 Kings 11:12)* but he may have been like any church kid in America today. He dragged his dusty Bible to church and back home, but it wasn't ever a priority to open up and learn for himself. Near the end of his copy of the law is a warning about following God, the blessings for obedience, and cursing for failing to heed Him.

Deuteronomy 28 is a fascinating chapter because it contains sixty-eight verses, of which only the first fourteen highlight the blessings of the people for following the law. The first verses of curses are enough to frighten the battle-hardened sinner into submission:

But it shall come about, if you do not obey the Lord your God, to observe to do all His commandments and His statutes with which I charge you today, that all these curses will come upon you and overtake you: "Cursed shall you be in the city, and cursed shall you be in the country. Cursed shall be your basket and your kneading bowl. Cursed shall be the offspring of your body and the produce of your ground, the increase of your herd and the young of your flock. Cursed shall you be when you come in, and cursed shall you be when you go out. The Lord will send upon you curses, confusion, and rebuke, in all you undertake to do, until you are destroyed and until you perish quickly, on account of the evil of your deeds, because you have forsaken Me (Deuteronomy 28:15-20).

Ultimately, we make decisions in our life and those decisions become the seeds for the fruit we will harvest by our deeds. If we are choosing daily to read, understand, and put into practice the things in the Word, our lives will reflect the blessing of following Jesus. But if we choose to follow our hearts and our fleshly desires, we will reap the rewards of worldly consequences.

Help Or Hindrance?

We all have friends from different walks in life. Some say we shouldn't even have non-Christian friends, but it is very possible to live a life close to God and have friends who do not believe. In fact, if all our friends are Christians, we may actually be doing things wrong. In this section, we will ask if our friends, Christian or not, help or hinder our walk with God.

The first type of friend we may find in our circle is the devoted Christian. These are the friends that are not merely *professors* of Christ, but *possessors* of the Spirit. We see them at church or a Bible study, and they are always more concerned with your spiritual walk than they are interested in the latest discussion of sports or politics. There is something about them that shows they know Christ more than merely professing to be saved by Him in the third grade. Their Bible is more covered in graphite and ink than dust.

Devout Christians sharpen each other *(Proverbs 27:17)*. When we meet together with people who are daily in the Word, we are encouraged into good deeds *(Hebrews 10:24)*. These are the people who can help us in our struggles *(James 5:16)* and they point us toward Christ. These friends draw us closer to God, and when we leave their presence, we devote ourselves further to Him.

The second type of friend we find in our circle are those who profess to know God, but it is pretty clear by their life they do not really believe in Him *(Titus 1:16)*. These friends are not true believers, but they follow God's innate nature to love. Most of them have the best intentions for us *(Matthew 5:46)*, but church is their social club and Bible study is the grueling task to get through in order to discuss other things. These friends are certainly nice people, but you know by observation that they rely on their wealth, knowledge, and skill rather than placing their confidence in Christ through faith *(Philippians 3:2-3)*.

In my experience, when we spend a lot of time around nominal Christians, we become frustrated. We need to walk a line between understanding someone may be a younger believer, but also recognizing that some people are deceiving themselves into thinking they are saved. When we meet a person who shows signs they are playing the Christian game without committing fully to Christ, we should focus our lives on encouraging them in faith and good works. Invite them to a private Bible study and see if you can spark their faith. On the flip side, if you allow them to speak into your life too much, they can pull you down and distract you from keeping your eyes on Christ. Take a warning from the author of Hebrews:

> *Therefore, since we have so great a cloud of witnesses surrounding us, let us also lay aside every encumbrance and the sin which so easily entangles us, and let us run with endurance the race that is set before us (Hebrews 12:1).*

Sometimes we find friends who are complete heathens and know nothing of Christ (and most of them don't even care for 'religion'). These friends may have been our best pals growing up, a co-worker who is otherwise pleasant to work with, or our neighbors. As I look back to most of the people I have known who lived lives in wanton pleasures, most were neighbors in the various apartments and townhouse complexes I have rented. Many of them were interesting to spend time with, though they were frequently a drain on my spiritual life.

In my experience, the best thing to do with such people is limit your time with them unless they are your specific calling from God. They are not the people I share my inner heart and struggles with. As we look to friends to give us advice, people who seek to solve their problems in a bottle rarely have solutions that will help us. These have been genuine friends whom I would help with house chores or drive to the store as needed, and we would share meals, but I always felt like a stranger in their lives. I believe, as Christians, we should feel like strangers in the lives of unbelievers. Peter wrote:

> *Beloved, I urge you as aliens and strangers to abstain from fleshly lusts which wage war against the soul. Keep your behavior excellent among the Gentiles, so that in the thing in which they slander you as evildoers, they may because of your good deeds, as they observe them, glorify God in the day of visitation (1 Peter 2:11-12).*

These friends who do not know God should be those with whom we share the Gospel, helping when we can show our commitment to good works *(Ephesians 2:10)* and never partaking in their sins they may do to ease their daily struggles.

We may also befriend an atheistic hater of the faith. Sadly, I was such a person to a friend when I was young. I had a friend who was raised in the church, and we often spent evenings in high school sipping coffee by the lake talking about all manner of topics. We had a standing rule: *We would not talk about God.* I didn't want to hear about faith, and he could not defend his God to my scientific and analytical mind.

My advice here is not to turn away from such a person as we shared a great friendship over the years, but as a Christian now, I will suggest that one such person can really rattle your faith. But such conflict is a means to strengthen your faith by finding the answers to their doubts. My friend held strong in the faith. While he could not defend his God against me, he kept praying for me. That is our lesson about friends who are hostile toward God. Just keep praying, not only for the friend but also for an answer why God sent them to you in the first place.

I am living proof that God can transform even the most hateful person in the world. While I stood on my pride as the smartest person I knew, and that I could easily shoot down all the arguments for God, He still saved me in the end. When you have a friend who is an atheist, the best thing to do is pray, and not let your faith be rattled from such arrogance. If you are interested in learning more about my story, have a look at my book, *Half My Life: How Jesus Conquered my Soul*[3].

A Life Well Lived

In the next chapter, we will explain what true salvation really looks like. Presently, however, I want to talk about what life looks like when we make Godly choices. Before we talk about that, we need to talk about an error in the church that has been creeping up lately: Hyper Grace.

The idea behind Hyper Grace is that God set us free from sin, and He has given us grace in accordance to our sin. The principle lends itself to an idea that God covers our sin. This is true, but many assume we can keep sinning because God's grace abounds *(Romans 5:20-21)*. I want to be clear that the people teaching this view of grace are generally not suggesting that we go out and actively sin on purpose. But they teach we do not need to concern ourselves with improving our life because grace abounds.

The error here is Scripture regularly challenges us to leave behind the worldly ways. The best example is the very next verses:

> *What shall we say then? Are we to continue in sin so that grace may increase? May it never be! How shall we who died to sin still live in it (Romans 6:1-2)?*

It is quite simple why these verses aren't often connected: chapter separations. We will remember that the chapter and verse divisions in our Bibles were placed only in the modern era. But when we connect the end of chapter five with the beginning of chapter six, we see Paul writes grace is enough to overcome even the greatest sinner, but we should never live our lives in the safety net of grace. It is always there to bridge the gap between the godly standard we are called to have and the human ability our flesh allows.

Paul instructs Titus:

For the grace of God has appeared, bringing salvation to all men, instructing us to deny ungodliness and worldly desires and to live sensibly, righteously and godly in the present age (Titus 2:11-12).

The grace we experience moves us outside our self-pity and to leave behind the sin that so easily entangles our life. Grace is not there to allow us to remain as we were called *(Romans 5:8)* but as the path to live a Godly life before Him. Paul writes to the Ephesians:

> *So this I say, and affirm together with the Lord, that you walk no longer just as the Gentiles also walk, in the futility of their mind (Ephesians 4:17).*

Once we are saved, it is our task to live out our life in Christ by doing good deeds *(Ephesians 2:10)*, and not maintaining our life as we lived it prior to Christ *(Romans 6:21)*.

A life in Christ is one that is dominated by good deeds, moral character, honest dealings, and peace of mind. When we follow sin, our hearts become troubled, and we may experience consequences of God. This is exactly what happened to Joash:

> *They abandoned the house of the Lord, the God of their fathers, and served the Asherim and the idols; so wrath came upon Judah and Jerusalem for this their guilt (2 Chronicles 24:18).*

On the contrary, when we choose to leave behind the old life and start following Jesus, we experience a lift off our shoulders *(Matthew 11:29-30)*. The life leaved in peace with God and man is a life that is free of stress and toil that accompanies conflict. Jesus's brother says it well:

But the wisdom from above is first pure, then peaceable, gentle, reasonable, full of mercy and good fruits, unwavering, without hypocrisy. And the seed whose fruit is righteousness is sown in peace by those who make peace (James 3:17-18).

Chapter Summary

At the end of our life we never have the option of blaming someone else for our sins. Even if we are raised in a pattern of dysfunction, sin, and error, we are still liable for our choices. The Bible illustrates again and again the **consequences for disobedience.** As we live, we all surround ourselves with people who can direct our decisions like Joash's friends did. **Are we careful about the people who influence our lives?** If you have not taken stock of your friends, do it today. Not that we need to jettison the ones who are not saved, but being conscience of the people who can speak into our lives is an important principle. Finally, **seek a life well lived** that is best defined as being at peace with God and man.

6
Real Salvation

And in that day
The mountains will drip with sweet wine,
And the hills will flow with milk,
And all the brooks of Judah will flow with water;
And a spring will go out from
The house of the Lord
To water the valley of Shittim.
Joel 3:18

Many people think they are saved but will find themselves excluded from the kingdom in the day of the Lord. Jesus gives us a stark warning:

> *Not everyone who says to Me, 'Lord, Lord,' will enter the kingdom of heaven, but he who does the will of My Father who is in heaven will enter. Many will say to Me on that day, 'Lord, Lord, did we not prophesy in Your name, and in Your name cast out*

> *demons, and in Your name perform many miracles?' And then I will declare to them, 'I never knew you; depart from Me, you who practice lawlessness (Matthew 7:21-23).'*

These verses should cause all of us to stop and ponder if the faith we have is real. This chapter will talk about what true faith and salvation look like.

Perseverance Of The Saints

Does the Bible teach that once a person is saved, they are always saved? This is an important question to ask considering the present discussion. We summarized hypergrace, and if we are always saved, would that mean that the hypergrace teachers are right? Also, if someone is "once saved, always saved" should we not use every pragmatic approach possible to get someone to say the sinner's prayer? After all, we must confess Jesus as Lord and we shall be saved as the verse goes *(Romans 10:9)*. These questions are actually in error and they lead us to another problematic doctrine that ravaged the church in the 1980s. This is commonly known as "Easy Believism".

In Easy Believism, since we are always saved when we pray the sinner's prayer, we need to cast off the old idea that people came to Christ privately. The idea was to do anything possible to get people to pray an easy prayer of salvation. The fruits of this teaching included a famous play that spread around the country scaring people into praying the "sinners prayer", many VBS curricula that sought to scare kids into praying during a watered down Gospel presentation, and many churches that focused on "felt needs" (pleasures) rather than the weightier matters of faith. No real ministration of the Gospel ever needed to be presented and the cost of becoming a Christian was never evaluated *(Luke 14:26-35)*.

I even had an encounter with evangelists of this persuasion as a child. Four of us were riding our bikes down the neighborhood streets when two young men stopped us near the intersection at the bottom of the hill. They were dressed nice, probably better than I was used to seeing in the heat of summer. They were friendly, and we thought they might ask us directions, but instead, they wanted to give us directions... to heaven. One of them spoke.

"Do you know if you'll go to heaven when you die?"

We four boys were in a row, I being furthest from the man talking. Each one of us responded in kind, "I don't know."

The hook dangled before us, and these missionaries were staring down a four-for-one salvation deal through our eight little eyes. Their training took over. "Do you want to be sure you will be in heaven when you die?"

"Yes, yes, yes," came in sequence.

Their eyes fixed on me, but the poor fools were unprepared for my answer: "I really don't care." At least I was honest.

All the training for handing out tracts assumed no one wanted to go to hell, and that everyone longed for heaven. I threw the man off his script, so his emotions took over.

"You know you will burn in hell forever if you don't make it into heaven," he replied, probably counter to his training.

"I don't believe in God, or heaven, or hell," I said back to him.

Thrown off, he left me as a burning branch in the fire. He turned to the other three boys, pretending he wasn't having this conversation. He said to them, "You can be *sure* you will go to heaven if you say this easy prayer. Do you want to say it?"

They said they would, and they closed their eyes. Even I said the words with them, and the missionaries declared our position in heaven. They handed us some Bible tracts and told us to find a good church. The missionaries walked off, rejoicing for the four souls they thought they just sprung from hell.

We immediately discarded the tracts on a nearby lawn, and none of us changed anything. Last I knew, one boy in our group became an experienced drug dealer, another came out as homosexual, caring nothing for God. The last person, to this day, remains a staunch anti-theist. This encounter, however, showed me the absurdity of some people's belief that merely reciting a few sentences can lead a person to heaven, provided there was such a place. We all had a good laugh at the encounter later[4].

While the Bible teaches we cannot lose our salvation *(John 10:28-30)*, there is a lot more about being saved than praying a single prayer. We cannot look back to a single point in time to declare our salvation, but, rather, we look to our regular pattern of life. This is why *James 1:12* says:

> *Blessed is a man who **perseveres** under trial; for once he has been approved, he will receive the crown of life which the Lord has promised to those who love Him.*

Paul also says the same:

> *Pay close attention to yourself and to your teaching; **persevere** in these things, for as you do this you will ensure salvation both for yourself and for those who hear you (1 Timothy 4:16).*

Christians are not those who said something once in their past. They are those whom live their lives for God that demonstrate salvation.

Real salvation removes from us all the old, foolish ways we used to walk in, and we instead start looking forward to the ways of God, which leads us to good works. Consider the admonition which Paul gave to Titus and his hearers:

> *For we also once were foolish ourselves, disobedient, deceived, enslaved to various lusts and pleasures, spending our life in malice and envy, hateful, hating one another (Titus 3:3).*

The person who is really saved is the one who recognizes the old, sinful ways in his life, abandons the foolishness, and instead longs for the word of God as a thirsty deer longs for the water brooks *(Psalm 42:1-2)*. The saved person recognizes the sin in their life and truly repents of that sin, calling on Jesus to save them. We are not saved by following the law *(Galatians 2:20-21)*, but true salvation leads us to follow the moral code God put inside us. This is not a works-based salvation, but out of our salvation is the desire and focus on following God in such a way that we naturally want to obey the moral law He places in us:

> *"But this is the covenant which I will make with the house of Israel after those days," declares the Lord,*

"I will put My law within them and on their heart I will write it; and I will be their God, and they shall be My people (Jeremiah 31:33)."

Dedication To God

As we examine what a Christian is from the explanation in the last section, we need to ask if Joash fully committed himself to God or if he was more committed to his way of doing things. While we saw Joash doing amazing things for God during the life of Jehoiada, he didn't put His Word at the center of his life. We see in his life the same type of living that a man shows when he "follows God" to put it in our modern vernacular. That means he gives a lot of lip service to the church, helps with the group service activities, attends all the required meetings, and counts several believers among his friends. But he is also following the coattails of a friend or a family member who keeps him in attendance. To contrast this, when all the people in our life disappear out of view, and we still find joy in attending church and reading the Bible, we have assurance of our salvation.

Joash followed all the commands that Jehoiada issued. Once the priest died, however, Joash showed his true colors. He stopped following God, gave up on the temple, and even the character of his interactions with the people seemed to change *(2 Chronicles 24:21)*.

Real dedication to God means that even when all our influences have left us, and it may seem that even God Himself leaves us, we still seek Him with all our heart. Consider what Job said after losing all his possessions, his fortune, and his children:

> *Though He slay me, I will hope in Him.*
> *Nevertheless I will argue my ways before Him*
> *(Job 13:15).*

A genuine believer is the person who stands strong, praising God even when the entire world collapses around them. That is exactly what will happen in the end times. The world will get worse and worse. To even profess to know Christ will place a target upon us. We will be tempted with the world's ways, and we even fall in love with the world at large *(James 4:4)*. But when all that happens, it is the faithful, dedicated people who will be saved *(1 Timothy*

4:16). The faith of the Thessalonians, as reported to Paul, encourages him:

> *For this reason, brethren, in all our distress and affliction we were comforted about you through your faith; for now we really live, if you stand firm in the Lord (1 Thessalonians 3:8).*

As Christians, our task is to stand firm for God in all circumstances, demonstrating our dedication by following His ways no matter if they take us to material blessing or death. That is dedication to God.

Love For The World

When we talk about love for the world, we need to distinguish between love for the worldly ways and love for the people in the world. James warns that people who love the world, meaning the worldly systems, hate God:

> *You adulteresses, do you not know that friendship with the world is hostility toward God? Therefore whoever wishes to be a friend of the world makes himself an enemy of God (James 4:4).*

James has in mind here the worldly systems; the pleasures and possessions that entangle us and distract us from God *(Hebrews 12:1)*. As believers, we need to cast off the entanglements of the worldly desires and meager possessions that we may turn our full attention on the path God places before us. This does not mean that we can have no pleasure in the beauty or the Godly things of the world. We are still given a lot of things for enjoyment, and the Christian needs to balance that *(Ecclesiastes 2:24-25)*.

So here when we talk about love for the world, we mean the people of the world. They do not have to be Christians for us to love them. We should love all our neighbors, our friends, and even our surrounding strangers. It is as Jesus explains:

For I was hungry, and you gave Me something to eat; I was thirsty, and you gave Me something to drink; I was a stranger, and you invited Me in; naked, and you clothed Me; I was sick, and you visited Me; I was in prison, and you came to Me (Matthew 25:35-36).

We should help in places we can help and serve in the places we can serve. Our motivation is to strive to make the world a better place through good works and ease suffering when we find it. We cannot heal the entire world, but we can help to alleviate some suffering we encounter to share the Gospel.

For the younger believers, the temptation here is to get rid of the old friends who still offer the party lifestyle. Young believers should not just shun their friends, because they need the Gospel, too. The challenge is to find ways to cast off the sinful lifestyle often shared between unbelieving friends without shipwrecking the friendship itself. It is not always possible, but we should strive to become God's influence in our old friends. Perhaps by us changing our ways, we will motivate others to follow God, too. Paul reminded Titus:

> *In all things show yourself to be an example of good deeds, with purity in doctrine, dignified, sound in speech which is beyond reproach, so that the opponent will be put to shame, having nothing bad to say about us (Titus 2:7-8).*

When our old friends see us living in a new light, we are preaching all the Gospel we need to preach. It is important that we live the life in the words of our Gospel, so hypocrisy does not put our friends off. Our character is the best Gospel we can preach. Consider

Real Salvation

Daniel. When his colleagues wanted to destroy him, they had nothing they could do except as it concerned his faith before God. They hatched a wicked plan that placed Daniel in the lions' den. When the plan failed to destroy him, they cast the wicked men into the pit, and Darius proclaimed the nation must worship the God whom Daniel served *(Daniel 6)*.

This is the lesson that Joash was missing. It does not tell us for sure, but the story of this king reminds me of the kid who is perfect in the presence of his Christian parents, but seeks every opportunity to sin once he is out of their sight. I can imagine that the young men Joash consulted once Jehoiada passed away knew before anyone that Joash was not really a part of God's kingdom. Once the final Godly influence in his life passed out of his influence, the true nature of his heart took over. If he were really saved, he would have kept doing what Jehoiada had taught him.

Chapter Summary

In this chapter, we considered the doctrine known as the **Preservation of the Saints**, which means once a person is saved, they are always saved. However, salvation is **more than merely saying a prayer** after a Gospel presentation. Our true salvation is not shown by what was done in the past, but rather, by looking at the regular decisions we make in our life. **Are we really dedicated to God?** Or are we keeping one foot in the world? Finally, we look at love for mankind as a marker of salvation. **A real Christian will work for God.**

Create Your Personal Plan

We are all influenced by our close friends and associates. It is also true that we have found a friend in Jesus, as the song goes. So this begs the question: are we as close to Jesus as we are to the rest of the friends who surround us? In this final chapter, we will create a plan to help us determine if our influences will lead us closer to God or if they are seeking to pull us down.

Questioning Your Salvation

Some people would scoff at the idea of questioning your salvation, but that is exactly what Paul instructs us to do:

> *But a man must examine himself, and in so doing he is to eat of the bread and drink of the cup. For*

he who eats and drinks, eats and drinks judgment to himself if he does not judge the body rightly (1 Corinthians 11:28-29).

If we don't examine our life regularly, we can fall into human entrapment, or we may actually deceive ourselves. Nothing is as dangerous as self-deception. *Matthew 7:21-23* shows the results of such self-deception:

Not everyone who says to Me, 'Lord, Lord,' will enter the kingdom of heaven, but he who does the will of My Father who is in heaven will enter. Many will say to Me on that day, 'Lord, Lord, did we not prophesy in Your name, and in Your name cast out demons, and in Your name perform many miracles? And then I will declare to them, 'I never knew you; depart from Me, you who practice lawlessness.

A healthy person in Christ will daily ask himself if he really loves God. It will be on the forefront of his mind as he weighs every decision that lay before him. Not that he is perfect, but a desire to follow God is the good first step.

All that being said, let me address the people who think they are unworthy of Christ. If you think you may not be saved because of how wretched you are, you are exactly where you need to be. Your feeling of unworthiness is exactly where a sinner needs to be as he prays to God. Consider the man who was too ashamed to raise his eyes to the sky:

> *But the tax collector, standing some distance away, was even unwilling to lift up his eyes to heaven, but was beating his breast, saying, 'God, be merciful to me, the sinner!' I tell you, this man went to his house justified rather than the other; for everyone who exalts himself will be humbled, but he who humbles himself will be exalted (Luke 18:13-14).*

God demands humility, and if you think you are not saved because of the sin you struggle with, you are wrong. It is exactly this humility that God blesses and then gives a greater grace. Paul struggled with similar thoughts:

> *For I know that nothing good dwells in me, that is, in my flesh; for the willing is present in me, but the doing of the good is not. For the good that I want, I do not do, but I practice the very evil that I do not want. But if I am doing the very thing I do not want, I am no longer the one doing it, but sin which dwells in me. I find then the principle that evil is present in me, the one who wants to do good. For I joyfully concur with the law of God in the inner man, but I see a different law in the members of my body,*

> *waging war against the law of my mind and making me a prisoner of the law of sin which is in my members. Wretched man that I am! Who will set me free from the body of this death? Thanks be to God through Jesus Christ our Lord! So then, on the one hand I myself with my mind am serving the law of God, but on the other, with my flesh the law of sin (Romans 7:18-25).*

The struggle we see in our lives between the person *God calls us to be* and the *person we are* is evidence that we are saved, because we are striving for the perfection, even though we will not get it on this side of heaven.

Focus On Prayer And Bible Study

Influence comes from spending time together. We are created to be in a community and to spend time with one another. When we spend that time with someone who is in close fellowship with God, we are drawn closer to Him ourselves. If our friends do not have a personal relationship with Jesus, we can be brought down with excess time spent with them. Both these examples, however, are friendship by proxy when we are considering our walk with Christ.

Our direct fellowship with God comes when we spend time with Him. He gave us the Bible to give us knowledge of who He is. We get into the mind of God when we read the Bible:

And do not be conformed to this world, but be transformed by the renewing of your mind, so that you may prove what the will of God is, that which is good and acceptable and perfect (Romans 12:2).

Our world talks a lot about Jesus, but often it is exclusive to the flowery ways of thinking about God. It is all about the feelings we have, and that is because our world has become dominated by feelings. But feelings are not the world of God. In fact, feelings can lead us astray. When we find a conflict between what we feel and what the Bible says, we need to follow the Bible. Peter tells us to be sober in mind and spirit:

Therefore, prepare your minds for action, keep sober in spirit, fix your hope completely on the grace to be brought to you at the revelation of Jesus Christ (1 Peter 1:13).

We cannot prepare our minds and be sober in spirit without the knowledge in the Bible. We need to read the Word regularly to understand the goals God has for us. The Bible is the window in the mind of God.

Prayer is also important. It is like listening to God. When we spend time in prayer, we are in fellowship with Him. We are seeking to let God inform us of the ways to apply the Bible to our lives. It is quite clear that the Bible is sufficient for us *(2 Timothy 3:16-17)*. But it does not address every aspect of our modern lives like what job should we pursue, who to marry, what church to attend, and more. To understand these, we need to read the Bible to learn what the guideposts are and then spend time in prayer with God seeking His will in these matters.

If Bible study gets us into the mind of God, then prayer gets us into the heart of God. When we spend time daily seeking God, we become more like Christ. Find time daily to create the practice of reading and studying the Bible. Begin or end each session with prayer and treat that time as holy, free of distraction. When we become more like Christ, we will inherently become people to challenge our friends in the faith. We will also lessen the impact that negative influences will have on our own minds.

Examine All Influences

The critical part of our plan will be to evaluate our influences. This is not to look at our friends and cut some loose. While there may well be reasons to release some people back into the pond of life, for the most part, we are interested here in how some people will influence us, so we can adjust accordingly.

The first myth we will bust here is that the purpose of evaluating friends is to let go everyone who is not a Christian. One problem many believers have is that they are so surrounded by other Christians they can't possibly fulfill the commandment to go into all the world to preach the Gospel *(Matthew 28:19-20)*. We should keep most of our current friends once we are saved. And we should also mention that every interaction does not need to turn into a Gospel presentation. Our friends should know where we stand with Christ and our activities with these friends should not violate the Scriptures. Just be sure that our non-

Christian friends are not influencing us to disobey the Bible. If we stop taking part in old activities because of following God, that is probably the time some of our old friends will leave us. This is like the discussion on marriage that Paul gives us:

> But to the rest I say, not the Lord, that if any brother has a wife who is an unbeliever, and she consents to live with him, he must not divorce her. And a woman who has an unbelieving husband, and he consents to live with her, she must not send her husband away. For the unbelieving husband is sanctified through his wife, and the unbelieving wife is sanctified through her believing husband; for otherwise your children are unclean, but now they are holy. Yet if the unbelieving one leaves, let him leave; the brother or the sister is not under bondage in such cases, but God has called us to peace (1 Corinthians 7:12-15).

The only people that we should cast off from being friends are the people who are outright toxic. This can come as toxicity toward the Christian faith, being a nasty person, or someone who leads us directly into sin. The toxic people we should excise because of faith disputes are not those who merely reject God, but those who are hostile toward Him. These friends insult

Create Your Personal Plan

us for our belief in God, and do whatever they can to put stumbling blocks before our feet. The Bible has some harsh words for such a person *(Matthew 18:6)*, so these are the ones with whom we should cease communication, but be careful not to slander them. Leave the judgment to God.

People who lead us into sin should also be deleted from our contact list. Once we have fallen into major sin with someone, we cannot return to Eden. As a young man just before meeting Jesus, I engaged in fornication with a woman. Sadly, she was a professing believer and the instigation of the sin. I freely participated in our evil acts, and once I became a Christian, my conscience bothered me about it more and more. After reading through the Bible and understanding the gravity of such sin *(1 Corinthians 6:18)*, I rudely walked out of this woman's life. I deleted her emails, removed the number from my contact list, and ignored every call she attempted to make. I knew that if I spent any time with this woman, sin was likely at the end of the night, and I didn't need that influence *(Romans 13:14)*.

Other friends may give us good counsel in life. These are the people that we should keep close, and also increase our time with them if possible. They may look for one-on-one time with another fellow believer, or perhaps you can look to start a Bible study together. When we find a good friend who can give us positive advice and counsel, we should heed the words they say *(Proverbs 27:17)*.

Seek Out Christian Service And Fellowship

Fellowship is best found in Christian service. When we are looking to bolster our friends and associates, like-minded Christians are the best new friends we can make. If we want to make friends with a drunk, we can hang out in a bar, but to find Christians, look for opportunities in and around the church. Christian service and ministry attracts people who love serving and following Christ, so answering opportunities to help the poor in the community through church outreach can be a great place to meet Christians.

If you think you may need to learn more about God before looking for opportunities to do good works, you will forever miss out on the good things God has in mind. As believers, we are zealous for good deeds *(Titus 2:14)*. In fact, God saves us to *do* good works:

For we are His workmanship, created in Christ Jesus for good works, which God prepared beforehand so that we would walk in them (Ephesians 2:10).

When we serve, we will grow in Christ by seeing the importance of Christ in our lives. Once we recognize the importance of Godly people surrounding us, we will have learned the final lesson that our influences are the most important thing in the evolution of our faith.

The Gospel

We have all sinned. In our natural condition, we perform actions displeasing to God. These actions are called sin, and since God cannot be in the presence of sin, we are, by our nature, separated from Him. If we die in this state, we are bound to eternal separation in hell. However, God provided a way out of our deathly state. Jesus Christ, who was fully God and fully man, lived on the earth, was tempted in all ways as we are, and lived a perfect life. Jesus willingly went to a cross and died for our sins so we would be able to be in the presence of God. This sacrifice by Jesus is a free gift that makes us clean before Him.

We take hold of this gift by prayer. We must understand and admit our sinful state, incapable of being able to resist sin. We must acknowledge Jesus has the power to cover our sin. Pray to God to receive Christ's sacrifice on your behalf, and you will be cleansed of your sin, both great and small.

If you have prayed to receive Jesus, mind the words in this book. Begin to read the Bible, search out Christian fellowship, and learn what God would teach you. Grow in faith and sanctification, cleanse your heart and submit to God's Word. Welcome to the kingdom.

Bibliography

1. The Good, The Bad & Butch, *Adventures in Odyssey*, Volume 23: Twists and Turns, Episode 4, 1995.
2. Under the Influence, *Adventures in Odyssey*, Volume 38: Battle Lines, Episodes 488, 489, 2002
3. Half My Life: How Jesus Conquered my Soul, Thomas Murosky, 2021, OWIC Publishing
4. I explain this story in more detail in *Half My Life, How Jesus Conquered My Soul* in the chapter, "I Don't Care If I Go To Heaven"

Scripture Index

New Testament......................
- 1 Corinthians 11.........82
- 1 Corinthians 15.........40
- 1 Corinthians 6...........89
- 1 Corinthians 7...........88
- 1 Peter 1......................85
- 1 Peter 2......................60
- 1 Thessalonians 3.......76
- 1 Timothy 4..........72, 75
- 2 Peter 1......................43
- 2 Timothy 3................86
- Acts 8..........................47
- Ephesians 2....60, 64, 91
- Ephesians 4.................64
- Galatians 2..................73
- Galatians 5.....16, 43, 54
- Galatians 6..................53
- Hebrews 10. .37, 44, 46, 57
- Hebrews 12..........58, 77
- James 1.......................72
- James 3.......................65
- James 4.....................75p.
- James 5.................37, 57
- John 10..................37, 72
- John 6..........................53
- Luke 14.......................69
- Luke 18.......................83
- Matthew 11................64
- Matthew 18................89
- Matthew 25................77
- Matthew 28................87
- Matthew 5..................57
- Matthew 7 11, 18, 68, 82
- Philippians 3..............58
- Romans 10..................68
- Romans 12..................85
- Romans 13..................89
- Romans 14..................37
- Romans 5.................62p.
- Romans 6.............62, 64
- Romans 7....................84
- Titus 1...................15, 57
- Titus 2......45, 63, 78, 91
- Titus 3........................73

Old Testament......................
- 1 Kings 11...................27
- 1 Kings 12.................35p.
- 1 Kings 16...................22
- 1 Kings 18...................22
- 1 Kings 19.............23, 25
- 1 Kings 22...................23
- 1 Samuel 22................27
- 1 Samuel 8..................27

2 Chronicles 14..........33	Genesis 12..................28
2 Chronicles 23..........32	Hosea 10.....................45
2 Chronicles 24...32pp., 49, 64, 75	Jeremiah 31................74
	Job 13........................75
2 Kings 11.........25p., 54	Joel 2....................21, 31
2 Kings 12.........31p., 49	Joel 3..............39, 51, 67
2 Kings 22...............23p.	Joshua 24...................51
2 Kings 8.....................24	Judges 21...................26
2 Kings 9.....................25	Micah 4......................31
2 Samuel 12................27	Micah 5......................39
Daniel 6......................79	Micah 6......................51
Deuteronomy 28.28, 34, 55	Micah 7......................67
	Proverbs 16................52
Deuteronomy 34.........26	Proverbs 22..................9
Ezekiel 23....................24	Proverbs 27..........57, 90
Genesis 11..................14	

Other Books by Thomas Murosky

Josiah's Sanctification
ISBN:
978-1-732569645 (s)
978-1-7325696-5-2 (e)

Lessons Learned From a Lost Book

Testing and Temptations
ISBN:
978-1-7325696-0-7 (s)
978-1-7325696-1-4 (e)

Do you know what it takes to live like Jesus?

I AM not amused
ISBN:
978-1-7325696-2-1 (s)
978-1-7325696-3-8 (e)

Does your entertainment honor God?

About Thomas Murosky

Thomas Murosky has a background in Biological Sciences earning his Bachelors in Biochemistry and his Doctorate in Molecular Toxicology. He taught Chemistry at Bucknell University and Western Wyoming Community College. While as a student and professor, Tom worked in several capacities as a children's and youth worker having served the local CEF board, as a counselor for Christian camps, Awana programs, and other youth outreach including a decade of work in Big Brothers, Big Sisters of America.

Tom stepped aside from teaching and academics to work as a technology consultant to focus more time on writing, blogging, and video production in the area of Christian teaching with an emphasis on discipleship and sanctification. His first book, Testing and Temptations, is about how we are called to transform our lives to be like Christ in the process of Sanctification. His second book, The Art of Shallow Neighboring is parody book calling us to better Christian discernment in the books we read. His third book, I AM Not Amused calls for sober analysis of the media entertainment industry. In addition to these, Tom produces videos on current Christian events and sound theology on OurWalkinChrist on YouTube.

You can find more information and other books Thomas has authored at www.ourwalkinchrist.com. Signup for the newsletter for information on future releases, promotions, and advance reader copies at https://newsletter.ourwalkinchrist.com/.

www.ingramcontent.com/pod-product-compliance
Lightning Source LLC
Chambersburg PA
CBHW060405080526
44583CB00012B/480